INTERNET SUCCESS

12 Secrets Revealed

INTERNET SUCCESS

12 Secrets Revealed

Madeleine Kay

Chrysalis Publishing

Published by:

Chrysalis Publishing
P.O. Box 675
Flat Rock, NC 28731

ISBN 10: 1463689543
ISBN 13: 978-1463689544
Printed in the United States of America

DEDICATION

To all my fellow techno-phobes
and techno-dummies . . .

There *is* hope!

BOOKS IN THE INTERNET SUCCESS SERIES

Whether you are a beginner on the computer, a techno-phobe, a novice computer or business person, a budding entrepreneur . . . or just someone who wants to create a successful business on the internet without "reinventing the wheel" or wading through the avalanche of information to learn how to do what you want, my new series of internet marketing books on the subject of internet success will help you discover how to create a successful internet business simply, easily, quickly and inexpensively.

This series includes the following books and will be available in both paperback and digital formats. Some books in the series may not yet be available, but will be shortly, so check back for these . . . and for other books that may be added to the series.

Internet Success for Beginners . . . 7 Secrets Revealed
(A guide for the true beginner)

Internet Success for Beginning Entrepreneurs
. . . 7 Secrets Revealed
(A guide for the novice entrepreneur)

Internet Success . . . 12 Secrets Revealed
(Combines both of the above *Internet Success*
books in one volume)

Millionaire Marketing . . . How to Make
the Internet Work for You
(A guide to some broad marketing concepts
for the internet)

ACKNOWLEDGMENTS

To my good friend and graphic designer
– Claire Collins –
without whom none of this would be possible.
Thank you so much!

And many thanks to Zaldy Icaonapo
for the sensational cover image.

BOOKS BY MADELEINE KAY

Serendipitously Rich . . . How to Get Delightfully,
Delectably, Deliciously Rich (or anything else
you want) in 7 <u>Ridiculously</u> Easy Steps

Living Serendipitously . . . keeping the wonder alive

Living with Outrageous Joy

The 7 Secrets to Living with Joy and Riches

The 12 Myths About Money

The UMM Factor
(what you need in order to succeed)

Coming Soon

How Will I Ever Get Over My Happy Childhood
(Short stories)

The Serendipity Handbook

Savoring Life . . . Not Just Working At It
8 Principles for Liiving a Delicious Life

Scats . . . scattered thoughts on just about everything

For information on *all* products and services –
books, e-books, e-courses, coaching, consulting,
"fun stuff". . . and more
visit www.madeleinekay.com

CONTENTS

Note from the Author ...17

Introduction ...19

PART I – For Beginners

Secret #1 ... 25

Secret #2 ... 31

Secret #3 ... 35

Secret #4 ... 39

Secret #5 ... 43

Secret #6 ... 47

FYI ... 49

A Note ... 51

PART II – For Novice Entrepreneurs

Secret #7 ... 57

Secret #8 ... 63

Secret #9 ... 67

Secret #10 ... 71

Secret #11 ... 75

Secret #12 ... 77

FYI ... 81

Afterword ... 83

About the Author ... 85

Other Books by Madeleine Kay ... 87

Links and Resources ... 91

Notes ... 97

NOTE FROM THE AUTHOR

This book combines my first two books in the *Internet Success* series on creating a successful internet business . . . and doing it simply, easily, quickly and inexpensively.

The two books combined in this volume are *Internet Success for Beginners* and *Internet Success for Beginning Entrepreneurs*. You can read each of these books by themselves, without reading the other, since each book is complete in itself. Or, if you want to read both books, you have the choice of reading them as two separate books . . . or as one, in this volume. All three of these books are, or will be, available as both digital books and paperbacks, so you can read them in whatever format most pleases you.

All the books in the series are written very simply and clearly, with information that is non-technical and simple enough for anyone to understand and be able to use.

It is my hope that by making the subject simple, clear and uncomplicated, you will realize that you actually *can* do this . . . and will.

EnjOy,

Madeleine

INTRODUCTION

After publishing my first book and working relentlessly for three years to get into all the traditional major distribution systems and venues, I realized that was not the way to go. Online was the way – a way I knew nothing about . . . and cared even less about, since I was a major techno-phobe.

Nevertheless, I forced myself to forge through the online world and spent the next three to four years doing what I liked least and learning about what I didn't even care for – the internet, computer sales and marketing . . . and that whole cyber-world.

By the time I learned what I needed to know and actually began to understand it so my head stopped spinning and I stopped getting dizzy every time I sat in front of a computer . . . everything had changed and the internet world had advanced and exploded.

Nevertheless, those three to four years of study helped me quickly learn and assimilate the new information and put it to practical use. (Probably because I used to have my own advertising, marketing and PR agency, so I managed to develop a huge amount of "stickiness" regarding the important things . . . the simple things . . . the fast and easy things about online marketing and making money in the internet world.)

Now, I want to share with you what I have learned – so you don't have to spend the agonizingly laborious three to four years that I did learning all this and assimilating it, so it actually becomes usable information, rather than just disorganized clutter in your brain.

I'm not going to talk about the most obvious or the very complicated, technical or expensive ways to succeed on the internet. There are plenty of books out there on those . . . and I imagine that most of you are not looking for complicated, expensive or technical. My guess is that most of you want simple, easy, fast and inexpensive . . . or even, free.

So, here goes – as simply and succinctly as possible – to help you get started creating your own internet business success. Here are 12 really simple, easy-to-do, inexpensive secrets I have learned about creating success online.

(Resources and links to what I have found to be the best, most helpful and inexpensive companies to help you, are listed throughout the book . . . and also, at the back of the book – *with phone numbers whenever possible*, for those of you who, like me, prefer to speak to a live person rather than getting your information from or asking your questions via e-mail. Most, but not all of these, are companies that I use, and have used for years.)

PART I

FOR BEGINNERS

Secret #1

CREATE AN AFFILIATE SITE
OR SITES

This can be done for practically no money at all . . . or even, completely free! (More about that later.)

You can do it for a $9.49 - $11.99 annual domain fee, plus $48 - $60 a year hosting fee for basic hosting . . . and that's it!

You can get your domain name and hosting at Go Daddy (www.godaddy.com) . . . and get your affiliates and get paid through ClickBank (www.clickbank.com), which has no up-front costs or fees . . . they only take a very small percentage once something has sold.

Let me explain the fees – which are ridiculously minimal – and explain what an affiliate site is.

As I said, ClickBank is completely free to sign up with and has no up-front costs. They make their money by taking a very small percentage (approximately 7.5% plus a $1.00 transaction fee) from what you get paid AFTER someone purchases something through your affiliate link.

What is an affiliate site? It's a site on which you list (and promote, if you wish) other people's products and services. All the products and services on ClickBank are digital, probably because those are the simplest, fastest, easiest and usually, the highest profit items to list, promote and deliver.

So you don't have to actually sell anything. You don't carry any inventory. You don't have to write, produce, create or distribute anything. You don't even have to write any sales copy. It's all done for you automatically. You are just the "middle man" (or "middle person") letting people know about it.

How do you let them know? By putting up a web page. I recommend putting it up on Go Daddy (www. godaddy.com). There are others, but I have used Go Daddy for ten years and have found them to be excellent. (Another one growing in popularity, that you might want to check out, is www.intuit.com, which is also simple and inexpensive.)

Go Daddy is an internet company for anyone and everyone – they truly offer internet services "for dummies," and techno-phobes. Their service is great! It's fast, simple and really inexpensive. Their service people are really knowledgeable and helpful – and are always available – 24/7!

So, you can buy any domain name that is

available, through Go Daddy . . . and even sign up for names that are not currently available, but will or may be coming available.

Once you get your domain name, you can use their simple templates to put up your site.

Once your site is up, you get affiliate links or banner ads (whichever you prefer) to put up on your site. Then, every time someone clicks on your link or banner and purchases one of those products or services, you receive a commission . . . often as high as 75% - 80% of the sale price.

Again, you do not have to deliver the product or service . . . or create it. You are merely providing a link, directing people to the website at which they can learn about it and purchase it if they wish to. If they do purchase, then you receive a commission just for connecting them.

How and where do you get affiliate links to or banner ads for these products and services? An easy way is to go to ClickBank (www.clickbank.com) and sign up as an affiliate. It's free!

Then go to their marketplace and just click on the categories and products and services you want to promote . . . and ClickBank will create what they call a hop ad for you to put on your website or web page . . . and that's it!

You can even do this without having a website or page! Remember I said you can create an affiliate business absolutely free? Well, if you don't want to buy a domain name . . . if you don't want to put up a web site or web page . . . you can still do this. How?

After you select the products or services you want to promote, ClickBank will create two things for you – one is the hop ad for your website or page (it is in html format) and the other is a hoplink – which is simply a text link that you can send out in e-mails to friends, family, associates, etc. By doing this via e-mail, you are in essence, creating your own affiliate business absolutely free . . . you don't even need a domain name or a website.

ClickBank will automatically calculate your commission and will send you monthly checks (once you submit your payment information to them) – within 60 days of purchase to allow for returns (since their return policy is 60 days).

It's as simple as that – fast, easy, simple, and inexpensive . . . even possible for absolutely free!

There are lots of other sites and places to find affiliates. Two others are PayDotCom (www.paydotcom. com) and Commission Junction (www.cj.com), which give you the opportunity to become an affiliate for physical products as well as digital ones.

I've used ClickBank and I know many people who have also used it. It seems to offer a wide variety of excellent affiliate options and is really simple to use and set up. I have not used PayDotCom, but it has grown very quickly and become very popular . . . and is certainly worth your checking out.

Commission Junction is a very well-respected affiliate program company that has been around for awhile and is quite extensive. It is used by a lot of individuals, as well as large companies, to promote their products and services and is definitely worth checking out. I found it a bit more complicated than ClickBank . . . and have not actually used it myself, although I know of many people who have.

(FYI – I believe Commission Junction requires you to have a minimum monthly dollar amount of transactions and it charges a dormant account fee, if you have not had any transactions for six months. If you do want to use Commission Junction, make sure you read their entire agreement before signing up. You should, of course, *always* read the entire agreement, all the rules, fees, etc. prior to signing anything with any company, individual or business.)

Secret #2

CREATE A DIRECTORY SITE

What is a directory site? It is merely a site that lists information about people or places that offer a particular product or service within a specific industry or subject area. The site directs people to these companies, places, individuals or sites, where they can find and get what they are looking for in a particular industry, region, state, area, subject, etc.

The nature and complexity or simplicity of your site will depend upon how much you know about computers and how much time you want to spend on the computer and setting up your site.

Simply pick an industry, subject, area, region or state that you want to focus on . . . and then find and list companies, services, products or individuals in that arena on your site.

There are many different ways you can do this and approaches you can take.

One way is to do this site similar to an affiliate site. The main difference is that the easiest way to do an affiliate site is for only digital and downloadable products and services, so you can find the affiliate links all in one or two places, if you want.

(Affiliate sites can also be for physical products, but then you usually have to search the internet to see who has an affiliate program and sign up for each one separately. It's time consuming and not nearly as effective or productive. Two of the exceptions to this, as I mentioned, are PayDotCom (www.paydotcom.com) and Commission Junction (www.cj.com), which let you sign up to become an affiliate for both physical and digital products – all in one place.)

With a directory site, you have more freedom to create one broad general site – and then create lots of sub sites for that . . . i.e. computers, then break that category down into regions, cities, products, etc. So each directory site you have can generate many mini sites that are more targeted ones. In this way, you can blanket a market and blitz the internet.

You can list the same places on several of your sites and then link them – the search engines love links. The more you are linked, the more the search engines pick you up . . . and the links connect people who go to one of your sites, to all your others.

You can even create a national directory site for different subjects, industries, etc. by zip code. Go to www.pizza.com to see what I am talking about (as of the date of this writing), but I imagine that would take a bit of tech savvy to set up.

So, how do you make money from a directory site? Several ways . . .

One way to make money is by listing companies, individuals and sites with affiliate links, so you receive a commission when a sale is made through your link.

A second way is to charge a listing fee, and I would recommend making it so affordable, that they feel they cannot pass it up . . . they feel – why not list on your site. Rather than making a large profit on individual sales and listings, make your profit in quantity of sales. Make people an offer they can't refuse! Charge your "listers" a monthly fee or a reduced annual fee, if they pay for the year in advance. Then give them a ridiculously discounted rate if they list on multiple sites of yours.

A third way to make money from directory sites is to sell advertising on your site. Again – make people an offer they can't refuse – offer them a ridiculous rate, and again, offer them annual and multiple site discounts.

The fourth way to make money from a direc-tory site is to have a monthly newsletter, which helps you create a data base. And . . . you don't even have to write the newsletter. Offer the opportunity to a different advertiser or "lister" each month. (You can also sell advertising in the newsletter . . . and/or sponsorships.) This creates loyalty and continuity from and for your advertisers, listers and mailing list members.

All of these things (listings, advertising, sponsorships, mailing list for newsletter) help you create a data base that adds real value to your business and your site. So, after you've built it up over a few years, you put the site up for sale and auction it off through companies like Sedo (www.sedo.com) or Go Daddy's Domain Name After Market (TDNAM at www.godaddy.com).

If you have a good domain name . . . plus income coming in from advertisers and listers . . . plus a database, you may be able to sell your site (or business) for a lot of money (just like people sell their businesses offline). The guy who owned pizza.com sold his site and domain name for $1.3 million in 2008 on sedo.com – and it's a relatively easy-to-create site!

Secret #3

SELL DOMAIN NAMES

This brings me to the third secret to making money on the internet. If you own good domain names . . . or for a relatively small amount, decide to purchase some good ones – then put them up for auction on Go Daddy's Domain Name After Market (TDNAM) site at www.godaddy.com or on Sedo (www.sedo.com) and sell the names.

You can put up a parked page that announces that the name is for sale . . . or you can even put up an actively functioning site and sell the name. Even if you have a website already up, you can auction off the name.

In addition to Go Daddy and Sedo, there are other

domain name management companies that do auctions – both online and offline. At the time of this writing, a company called Oversee (www.oversee.net) and Snap Names (www.snapnames.com, a division of oversee.net) held a live auction in Fort Lauderdale, Florida which netted a total of $2,386,550 for 35 domain names. One of them, www.dating.com sold for $1.75 million – the highest bid among the 120 names up for sale at the DomainFest live auction. All the names that were not sold at the live auction, were added to an extended online auction.

Just think of websites as online real estate. That's what they actually are. Websites and domains are the new real estate . . . and online and the internet are the new property locations.

Be careful to read all the rules, regulations and small print when selling or auctioning off your site or domain name. There are several different kinds of auctions – you can declare a reserve amount below which you won't go (and if someone offers an amount equal to your reserve, I believe you must sell it then). You can put it up under "make an offer." There are 7-day auctions and 30 and 90 day auctions. There are premium listings you can pay for so your listing gets noticed more.

So, if you do decide to sell or auction your sites or domain names, make sure you have read and understood all the terms, responsibilities, caveats, binders, and whatever else there is in the small print. It can get very complicated, very competitive, very exciting . . . and of course, there are a lot of legalities involved. So read everything thoroughly, carefully . . . and always consult with your business, investment, financial, legal advisor before doing or signing anything.

Secret #4

CAPITALIZE ON PUBLIC DOMAIN PRODUCTS

Use public domain material for your site. What does public domain mean? It means that no one holds the copyright on it.

There are many public domain books out there that you can download from a variety of public domain sites like www.gutenburg.org . . . and then sell them on your site for $.99 each. Believe me the $.99 adds up – look at iTunes and the Dollar Stores!

You can do this with books . . . and also with photographs. There are a lot of magnificent government photos on space, nature, etc. However, it's a lot more work to upload photo images and create a site with high quality downloadable images, than it is with text products.

The service you are providing that makes it worth the $.99 to people – is convenience. They don't have to go to all different public domain sites to find what they are looking for . . . you've already done that for them. Of course, you don't call your site a public domain site . . . and it is your choice whether to mention that what you are offering is in the public domain. I suggest being up front about it and letting people know exactly what they are getting and that you are merely charging for the convenience of having done all the legwork for them and of having it all in one place for them.

Be sure to check the copyright information on all public domain books. Anything published prior to 1929 is in the public domain. But after 1929, it gets tricky because there are different copyright coverage periods and rules after that, so go to www.copyright.gov to check it out completely.

Also, if you are offering translations of foreign works (the original work published prior to 1929, but the translation after), make sure to check out whether that translation is, in fact, in the public domain.

Another service you are offering by doing this is bringing a lot of these older great and/or little known books to the public awareness and helping to make them popular and accessible again.

A Note . . . Just Google "public domain books". . . and a lot of sites will come up, from which you can learn about and get information on public domain books and download them. Always be sure to check the freedom of usage information on each site for the public domain books you download . . . and/

or any public domain products you wish to sell or offer, to make sure they can be resold commercially.

Secret #5

SET UP A STORE AT CAFE PRESS

If you are an artist – or a writer – and have either great ideas and/or images that you want to put on different products, but you don't want to carry inventory, or be responsible for producing and manufacturing the products, or be responsible for delivery or order taking or fulfillment – Café Press is ideal for you. (www.cafepress.com)

It is a very popular, international site that allows you to place your unique and individual sayings, ideas, logo and art work on hundreds of products to sell. It doesn't cost you anything to do this . . . the cost of producing each item is deducted from the sale price, *after* someone orders and purchases it. So there is no out-of-pocket cost to you to create, produce or sell these items.

Café Press has two kinds of stores that you can set up – Basic and Premium. The Basic Store is completely free to set up and a great way to start to build up inventory and customers. Of course, it is more limited than the Premium Store, in terms of what you can offer and how you can set up and customize your store.

The Basic Store allows you to offer only one of each item . . . and you cannot customize the appearance of your store. But as I said – it's free – and a great way to start, until you have both a customer and a product base.

The Premium Store costs $6.95 per month (or $18.45 if you pay for 3 months in advance, $34.95 if pay for 6 months, and $59.95 if you pay for a year) – and it lets you completely customize the appearance of your store . . . and you can offer as many different variations on, or sayings and images on or for, each item.

Their retail base price is very high however, so your mark up on each item will probably not be that great. But, since each item is custom-printed, people are willing to pay the higher prices if they like your saying or image . . . and . . . you will make your money, hopefully, in volume, rather than having a big profit margin on each item.

Also – it's a great way to get your name, product, service, ideas, images and your "branding" out there. Think of it as free advertising. Not only is it free . . . you get paid for putting your "brand" out there and on those products for people to buy, use, wear and enjoy.

And . . . Café Press even has an affiliate program.

So, you can be an affiliate and promote other people's products . . . and they can be affiliates and promote yours.

(Another site growing in popularity that allows artists and crafts people to sell their products is www.etsy. com. You sign up for free and can customize your shop. Then it costs only $.20 per item to list it for four months. When it sells, you pay a 3.5% transaction fee. Something you might want to check out.)

Secret #6

CREATE SUB-CATEGORIES
AND SUB-SITES

For just about all of these secrets – once you've created one or two main sites, you can easily create a plethora of sub sites. I touched on the subject a bit while explaining Secret #2 – Creating a Directory Site.

You can do this with directory sites, affiliate sites, public domain products sites . . . even your Café Press stores

You can literally break any broad, general category site into specific smaller sub sites – using the same templates – and often, a lot of the same listings.

For example – the broad category of computers can be broken down into ink cartridges and toners, printers, screens, service, retailers, etc . . . and then these can be broken down into regions, states, cities, etc.

So one site can generate many – each linked, sometimes with some overlaps, all of which help you establish a real presence on the internet and the search engines . . . and kind of blitz the internet and dominate a category, to a certain degree.

Or you can really diversify and have just one site in each of a multitude of different categories to cover and hit all different segments of the internet market.

Again, it's your choice how you want to go – wide and broad, or in-depth and specific.

FYI . . .

LINK ALL YOUR SITES

To exponentially multiply the reach and scope of your sites, you can link all of them.

The search engines love links . . . and the more your sites are linked, the more the search engines pick them up more easily. And . . . the more easily people on the internet find and get to all your different sites.

And the linking is not just limited to within each type of site. If you decide to do affiliate sites, directory sites, public domain sites, Café Press stores, or develop sub-sites of any or all of these, you can link all of them – and in that way, really cross section the internet market . . . and optimize your exposure and sales possibilities.

Linking is very easy to do. You can put up a Links and Resources page (or if you prefer, call it a Recommendations page) on your website(s), and on that page, just list the different website names, providing a link for people to click on and be taken to that site.

Or you can write a short blurb describing each of the different sites you are linking to (in addition to providing a link to get to it) . . . or, if you prefer, you can even create an image (or take images from the various sites) and post them on your Links and Resources (or your Recommendations) page . . . with a short blurb next to each image, describing the site and letting people know what it offers when they click on the link you provide. Since this is all done on the internet, always make sure you provide a live link for people to click on to be taken to the other site(s).

A NOTE

You'll be happy to know that you can implement most of these 7 secrets – your affiliate sites, directory sites, public domain sites, Café Press stores, and sub-categories – without having to pay for separate hosting for each one or without having to purchase a lot of different domain names.

Again, I am going to use Go Daddy (www.godaddy. com) as the model because it is truly the only company that I – as a recovering techno-phobe and techno-dummy – use and am absolutely thrilled, delighted and satisfied with. They are so helpful, reliable, always available, make their products and services easy to use and set up, and are ridiculously inexpensive.

So – if you don't want to purchase a lot of different domain names, but do want to set up a lot of different sites, you can get their economy hosting for $4.99 a month (or $47.88 a year), less any coupon or "Deal of the Day" discounts they are offering. Use one main domain name like uronline.com and then just add each separate page or category as an indexed page (ie: www.uronline. com/computers). As you create subcategories under that, just add another forward slash (/) . . . or for different categories, replace the word "computers" with the new category word.

Or, if you already have a lot of domain names – or want to purchase several and use them – you can purchase Go Daddy's deluxe hosting for $7.99 a month (or $83.88 a year). Remember to ask for the "Deal of the Day" or any coupons or discounts they are offering, which are usually from 15% to 25%. (The advantage of the deluxe hosting is that it has 150 gigs, while the basic has only 10 gigs . . . so you can host multiple domains for the one hosting fee.)

To host multiple domains, you just put each separate domain name up as a separate folder under that one main hosting account. Go Daddy will guide you to, through, and with the instructions on how to do this, if you have any difficulty. (You can also index pages with the deluxe hosting, just as you can with the economy hosting).

So, whichever way you choose to go, you are only paying for hosting once, even though you are putting up a lot of different pages, websites, or domains.

The main thing is to keep it as simple and inexpensive as possible, at least at the beginning, until you develop more computer savvy, a larger customer base, and a momentum. Each of these secrets is simple, easy and expandable. They can be kept as simple as you choose . . . or be developed, elaborated and expanded as much as you want. The choice is yours.

The easiest, simplest and least costly way to set up a payment system – if you are not getting paid by ClickBank, Commission Junction or PayDotCom, is to set up a Pay Pal account. (www.paypal.com) It's free to set up and they only take a small transaction fee and percentage out of every payment . . . that's all!

PART II

FOR NOVICE
ENTREPRENUERS

Secret #7

WRITE AND SELL E-BOOKS

The publishing industry is changing so rapidly, that it is now easier, faster and less expensive than ever to write something and sell it.

E-books . . . or digital downloadable books used to be frowned upon by the mainstream publishing industry. Now, they are embraced and offered by many, if not all, of the major publishing companies and authors.

E-books just provide another way for people to read books. In this electronic age, digital is currently the fastest growing segment of the publishing industry.

There are so many benefits to publishing your book(s) digitally . . . that it could be an entire book in itself, which I will probably write to help guide people through the whole writing/publishing process with concise, simple, practical information about e-publishing and self publishing. But in the meantime, if you need assistance, I will be glad to personally coach you. Just go to my website www. madeleinekay.com to contact me.

But for our purposes here, let me just highlight the major points about and benefits of writing and selling your own e-books.

Because e-books are digital, they allow you to sell what you've written almost immediately after writing it.

Plus, you don't have to hire a graphic designer to design and create a cover. You don't need to hire an editor or book designer . . . or someone who is computer savvy enough to use InDesign or PhotoShop – both of which are usually necessary for preparing a book for traditional print publication.

Since e-books are digital, you can make changes or updates to them whenever you want (as often as you like or is necessary) after they have been completed and published. These changes can be made quickly and easily . . . and can include editing, adding things, deleting things, changing web sites mentioned and linked to, updates, etc.

In addition, if you have a website (or websites) and/ or other things to sell, you can insert live links into the document which, when clicked on, will take the reader directly to that site, without closing the e-book!

E-books can be sold very inexpensively – or for a lot of money – depending upon your subject, expertise, the length and complexity of the book, etc. If you make your e-book available only on your own website and not through any distributors or retailers (which is a whole other book, since it is too complex and too much of a digression to get into here), then you can literally set whatever value you want on your book, since the only way and the only place people can get it is directly from you – at your site.

Keep in mind that if you sell your book for very little, you generally do not need to write any sales copy, other than a paragraph or two describing the book. And, you don't have to gather testimonials or concern yourself about returns. Unless the book is really bad and does not deliver, no one is usually going to bother to return a $7 e-book or a book under or around $15 . . . so you don't usually have to deal with returns.

This is a good price if the e-book is between 30 to about 80 pages. Once it begins to be a longer book, then $7 to $15 might cause people to question the value of the book if it is priced too low.

Once the book is longer and higher priced however, you have to then write sales copy for it, put up a sales page to sell it, get testimonials, deal with returns, etc. So for now . . . for our purposes in this book, let's just talk about e-books that are between 30 to 80 pages. Let's keep it simple and easy.

My advice is – "Don't be greedy," since e-books are 100% profit (or almost 100%, since there is no, or very little overhead, especially if you sell them on a free website or a blog or through your e-mail). Take to heart the lesson of Wal-Mart – and be content to make your profit (at least, at the beginning, especially if you are a novice) on volume, rather than on the mark-up on each item. Things that offer buyers a real value and deliver more than expected can become viral on the internet very quickly!

You can sell your e-books on inexpensive hosted websites. The one I have been using for ten years now is Go Daddy (www.godaddy.com). Their economy hosting is $4.99 a month or if you pay the year in advance, it is $60. Be sure to ask about their "Deal of the Day" or special coupon discount offers, which are usually between 15% to 25%.

For more in-depth information about hosting on Go Daddy, you can refer to Part I of this book.

Another company that offers inexpensive and simple set-up hosting and support is Intuit at www.intuit.com. Their hosting is also $4.99 a month. They started up a few years ago, but have grown very rapidly and are very popular. I have no feedback or direct experience with them, but from what I have heard, their services and prices are similar to Go Daddy's and they are worth checking out.

I can however, tell you that Go Daddy is fabulous. It is truly an internet company that makes it possible for anyone to set up an internet business quickly, easily, simply and inexpensively. Their service is great. They are knowledgeable, helpful, speak to you in language you can understand . . . and they are available 24/7!

So, getting back to e-books . . . I'm suggesting beginning easily by writing a 30-80 page double-spaced e-book and selling it for $7 - $15. This way, the price stays low, the writing time is minimal, the writing should be easy because you focus on just one thing (or one aspect of a larger subject), and you type it in Word and make a PDF of your Word document . . . and you sell it.

If you write a few of these, each on a specific area of a larger subject; then you can combine them into a larger e-book and sell it for more. (But remember, then you probably need to put up a sales page for it, write sales copy and get testimonials.) You can even eventually combine the smaller e-books into a larger book and print a physical book. (More about that in Secret # 12)

To avoid any up-front costs, you can set it up so people purchase and pay for your e-books through Pay Pal (www.paypal.com), which accepts all credit cards. You do not pay Pay Pal anything until you sell a book . . . then they take a 2.9% commission of each sale, plus a $.30 transaction fee for domestic sales and a 3.9% commission, plus $.30 transaction fee for international sales. It's very simple.

You can also sell your e-books through PayDotCom (www.paydotcom.com), ClickBank (www.clickbank.com), Commission Junction (www.cj.com) . . . or other companies, but then it gets more complicated and a bit more costly. (Often, the cost is minimal or a one-time fee). But to keep things fast, easy, simple and free to begin with, you can start with Pay Pal. As you get more savvy and create more e-books and build a customer base, you can always upgrade to a more sophisticated or expansive system that offers you more options and services.

FYI . . . In addition to selling your e-books on ClickBank, PayDotCom and Commission Junction, you can also make them available for affiliates to sell and promote. (This subject is covered in more detail in Part I of this book.)

Secret #8

CREATE AND SELL E-COURSES

An e-course is great because it offers another venue for writers . . . and . . . a venue for people who are not writers, but have valuable information they want to share.

Once you've written your e-book, or a series of books, you can convert them to an online course. Or . . . you can develop the course without ever writing a book. (And maybe even, once you've developed the course, you will find that writing a book from it is easier than you thought.)

What is an e-course? It is simply a course that is delivered online through downloadable venues. You can deliver it by e-mail or on a special web page. (More about that later.)

Your course can be all text that is downloadable

each week (or each day) . . . or it can include audio (MP3, which is downloadable) or video (if you are more computer savvy) components, as well as free bonus gifts of products and services. These can be your own products or services or those of others who have given you permission to offer theirs as a free bonus gift. (More about that in Secret #10).

Creating audio and video components for your courses online is now easier, faster, and less expensive than ever . . . and sometimes, doesn't even cost anything. (More about that in FYI, at the end of this section.)

It is always best to offer as many free and different kinds of added value components and bonuses as you can with your course . . . so the person who signs up for it receives way more than just the value of the course itself. Depending on what additional items you offer, these bonuses and added value items are often more (or at least as) compelling as the course itself. These bonuses can be – other things you've written or produced or created; audios of interviews you've given; videos or DVD's of you; digital products you've created, like calendars, sayings, weekly or daily tips or inspirations . . . or some of the other things we will be talking about in Secrets #10 – #12.

Also – depending upon how tech savvy you are and how much work you want to do, you can even convert your online course to a home study course – which means you transcribe or print it all out and put it in a nicely presented looseleaf binder; you create CD's out of the MP3 audios; you include all the bonuses, and send a nicely presented package to the person. For this, of course, you charge a lot more than for the online course.

In the early days of internet marketing, online

courses often sold for $2000 to $3000 with very few extras. Now – people are so used to getting so much for free on the internet . . . those same courses probably will sell for $29 to $99 . . . including audio and/or video components, plus at least 7 to 10 free bonus gifts – usually many, many more.

Depending on what your course offers however, you may be able to sell it for a lot more. Especially, if your course is going to really help people change their lives, make money, get out of debt, create and build a business, etc. Courses offering very real-life, practical solutions are highly sought after and always in demand.

Unless you want to have to personally deliver the e-course manually through your own e-mail each week, you will probably need to sign up with an automated e-mail delivery system. One of the best, most reputable, reliable, simplest and least expensive I have found is AWeber (www. aweber.com).

The way it works is . . . once someone signs up for and pays for your e-course, Pay Pal (or whoever you use) sends a message to AWeber, telling them to begin delivering the course. Setting it up is a bit confusing for me because I am so "non-techi," but if you have any tech savvy, you can probably do it. If not, the people at AWeber and Pay Pal are very helpful . . . or you can probably pay someone $50 to set it up for you. AWeber charges $19 a month for this basic e-mail delivery service . . . or you can pay for longer periods of time and receive discounts.

You can also sell your e-courses on ClickBank, Pay-DotCom and Commission Junction . . . just as you can your e-books on these sites. And in addition to selling them, you can also make them available for affiliates to sell and promote. (This subject is covered in more detail in Part I of this book.)

Secret #9

CREATE AND WRITE A BLOG AND USE SOCIAL NETWORK SITES

Have you seen or heard of the film *Julie and Julia*? Well – that all began as a blog!

Julie was an unknown low-level employee of the 9-11 committee helping families of the victims of 9-11. She was bored and frustrated with her life and decided to begin writing a daily blog for one year about her adventures in cooking – her efforts to make every one of Julia Child's recipes in her book *The Joy of Cooking.*

After writing her frustrations, her innermost thoughts and feelings for a few months (it seemed to be almost like a journal or diary), she discovered she had gads of people following her blog.

Well – from her blog – she garnered a film, a book

67

. . . and a whole new life and career. All from a blog! How amazing is that?!

And blogs are free . . . so you can get, set up and run a blog for no money at all . . . and through that, create a brand, a following, a business and a presence on the internet.

Two sites that offer relatively simple, easy and free ways to set up a blog are Blogspot (www.blogspot.com also known as Blogger www.blogger.com) and WordPress (www.wordpress.com). I've been told by people who have used both, that BlogSpot is a bit simpler and easier for complete beginners.

Social networks are also free . . . and not only allow you to do much of what a blog does, but the exposure they provide is multiplied exponentially. Plus, social networks help create online communities that cross all borders, boundaries and physical limitations. They allow people to share, comment on, and disseminate information no matter where they are, who they are or what their situation is.

And – not only is social networking free – it is multi-media. So . . . it offers the opportunity for people to share, communicate and market themselves, their product or service in a multitude of ways – audio, video or text.

Social networking sites like YouTube, FaceBook, MySpace and Twitter have launched many careers and unknowns into the limelight who might never have been otherwise. The exposure they offer is huge, the potential for that exposure to go worldwide and viral is expansive, and the diversity of ways to express yourself on these sites is exciting and constantly expanding – from straight text and the written word, to audio, to video, to virtual simulcasts, to who knows what next! The possibilities seem to be endless

. . . and the opportunities are too!

There are also specialized social networks for just about every area of interest and targeted markets, industries and subjects. For example, for writing and business there are Linkedin, FiledBy, MeetUp, Diggit, etc. . . and the list goes on and on and is continually expanding. And you can use these social network sites . . . and blogs . . . to link back to your site, product or service. Just Google your area of interest or expertise to find the appropriate social networks for it.

These sites offer outlets and venues for you to showcase, announce, expose, and market yourself, your product or service. They offer the best PR you can imagine – and it's all free!

Secret #10

FIND JV PARTNERS AND AFFILIATES

What is a JV partner? It's a joint venture partner – someone who is willing to help you promote and market your e-book, e-course, product, or service (or even your physical product or service) in exchange for some benefit to them . . . which is often, just the opportunity to be exposed to your mailing list and that of others.

It's a little bit like the old barter system – except it's online . . . which is the new business, commercial, social, communications and living arena.

The beauty of JV partnering is that it doesn't cost anything. Like most of the things I have been recommending – it can be done for free!

It is usually done via e-mail. You contact people

who you want to JV partner with you – tell them what you have to offer and why and how it will benefit and be of interest to their mailing list, plus tell them how JV partnering with you will benefit them, their business and their career.

Usually the benefit is in their offering a free bonus for you to offer when you market or sell your product – so that gets their name and one of their products out to people on your mailing list . . . and those of everyone else who JV partners with you.

This works best, of course, if your product is either digital or it is sold on the internet, so you can put up a sales page to sell it and let people know all the free bonus gifts they will receive when they purchase your product.

Then you put up a "thank you page" to which they are directed after they purchase your product or service and at which they can download all their free bonus gifts.

Your JV partners also usually agree to send out a promotional e-mail to their list, recommending your product or service. To make things as simple and easy for them as possible, you usually write this e-mail and send it to them, so they can just paste it into their e-mail (making whatever changes they desire) . . . and then just send it off to their list. Also, hopefully they will post the same message on their blog, as well.

So the benefit to your JV partners again – is exposure to people on others' mailing lists to whom they would normally not be exposed, and the opportunity to have these people check out and try one of their products or services for free. It's basically having the advantage of being personally introduced to the people on the different mailing lists.

A corollary of JV partnering is to get others to sign up as affiliates to sell your product or service. If your products are digital, it's easy. Just go to ClickBank (www. clickbank.com) and sign up as a vendor. There is a one-time $49.95 fee when you activate your vendor account to sell something on ClickBank. Once you do that, the products you sell through ClickBank are automatically listed in their marketplace, so people who sign up as affiliates on ClickBank, know your product or service is available for them to promote.

You usually offer 50% to 75% commission. I know that may sound like you are giving a lot away – but not really, because those are sales you would not have had in the first place. So actually, you are making 50% to 25% on each sale on which you give those commissions . . . it's found money – and . . . it's free advertising and distribution for your name, product and service!

Two other good affiliate sites are Commission Junction (www.cj.com) and PayDotCom (www.paydotcom. com). You can sign up with one, two or all three of these (not for the same product, I don't think). ClickBank is the simplest to navigate and use and is for digital products only; PayDotCom and Commission Junction let you get affiliates for both digital and physical products.

Both ClickBank and Commission Junction have been around for awhile. PayDotCom is much newer. Commission Junction is a very large company and seems to be very reputable. (I have never used it because it is a bit more complicated and involved than ClickBank and I like to keep things simple.) PayDotcom has grown very rapidly and become very popular.

All of these companies automatically calculate the commission and your affiliates' monthly checks (after 30, 60 or 90 days, depending upon their return policy) – so you don't have to do any of that.

They all take out small fees for the service and then calculate the affiliates' and your vendor percentages.

Secret #11

OFFER COACHING AND TELESEMINARS

Everyone has areas of interest about which they know more than other people – things for which they have a passion – and they may not want to write a book or an e-book, or design and give an e-course on it.

Or . . . in addition to writing a book or an e-book, or offering an e-course, you may discover that you like or find your strength in and enjoy more direct contact with people . . . more interaction.

So you can take your area of expertise and interest and begin offering teleseminars and/or coaching. Both of these – as so many of the other secrets in this book – can be set up at no cost to you. There are many free conference calling services (one of which is www.freeconferencecalling.com

or you can Google to find others) through which you can set up your teleseminars – and even have them recorded and receive downloadable MP3's of the seminar (and some even allow you to edit the audio) – which you can then sell, make a CD of, have transcribed to sell, or even make into a book or a series of books and courses and other products.

In fact, when giving teleseminars, it is a great idea to ask people who have signed up for your teleseminar to e-mail you their most pressing question about your topic. In this way, you ensure that you are giving people the information they want . . . and . . . you are also gathering information that could be used for a book or an e-course.

You can also offer one-on-one or small group coaching and mentoring on your area of expertise and interest. Once you gain confidence, you can even submit your audio to booking agents, companies and sites that book speakers for conferences and other gatherings and venues. Public speaking is a very lucrative field, and giving teleseminars is a good way to begin.

Secret #12

OPEN AN ACCOUNT WITH CREATESPACE

CreateSpace (www.createspace.com) is for everybody who has a book, audio or video they've created and want to sell.

Book publishing, music production, audio and video production have been made so easy, simple, fast and inexpensive – it's mind boggling. And . . . the distribution – which used to be a major hurdle – is now part of the whole package, which is very inexpensive . . . and sometimes, free!

Print on Demand has become highly respectable and acceptable now and the companies offering it are often quite good . . . and they offer you packages, usually from $299 to $499 to help you get your book into print – to set up your title in their system, send you a proof, and give you tech support. They will also often advise and help you every step of the way.

For example, check out Infinity Publishing (www. infinitypublishing.com) for their publishing packages. I have friends who have used Infinity's publishing services and were very satisfied. You can even get the service for $115 ($75 set up fee and $30 for the proof copy) at Lightning Source (www.lightningsource.com), which is the Print on Demand division of Ingram – the largest distributor to bookstores.

But the best deal of all is at CreateSpace (www. createspace.com) – Amazon's Print on Demand division. CreateSpace offers you the opportunity to create books, CD's, DVD's, etc. – and sell them all on Amazon – all for free!

There are no up-front costs at all – and – you get distribution on CreateSpace and Amazon. Amazon usually takes a 55% distributor's percentage, but if you produce your book through CreateSpace, they only take 40%. So your royalty is 60% of the retail price, minus the cost of producing each item once a customer orders it.

You also have the option of paying a one-time fee of $39 (then $5.00 annually per enrolled title) to get your book into their Expanded Distribution System and have it available in all bookstores and online venues. When it is sold through these expanded distribution outlets, the distribution discount is 55% plus the cost of producing the book. But – by signing up for the expanded distribution – the cost of producing your book goes down substantially.

(As of this writing, I do not believe the expanded

distribution is available for audios and videos. You do however, receive a bulk discount if you purchase 50 or more of your own audios and videos for you to distribute. But check with CreateSpace on this since they are always expanding and improving their services.)

If you have any question, go to www.createspace.com and click on Contact Us. Then you can either e-mail them and they will e-mail you back, usually within 24 to 48 hours . . . or you can request that they call you, which they will literally do the second you click on "call me."

It's a fabulous service . . . and it lets all kinds of artists and creative people (not just writers) produce and sell their work with no up-front costs. How great is that?*!

And . . . if you do want or need someone to help you with the formatting or design, they also offer inexpensive packages and help.

FYI...

CREATE AN AUDIO OR VIDEO

CreateSpace is as good a venue and outlet for musicians and filmmakers who want to produce and distribute their audios and videos, as it is for writers. You can create and distribute your audios and videos through CreateSpace . . . or on a multitude of growing venues on the internet.

The internet is expanding so rapidly that now offering text or the written word only is just one small part of what people expect, want and are willing to pay for.

With cell phones that take high quality photographs; with companies like CreateSpace that let you produce and distribute your audios and videos worldwide with no up-front cost to you (or minimal, if you need and choose to pay for production and design assistance); with social media like YouTube, FaceBook,Twitter and all the others available and those yet to come . . . the possibilities for making money on the internet are endlessly diverse.

If you can get your YouTube video to go viral and get upwards of half a million or a million hits, YouTube will actually contact you about selling advertising on your page, so you can monetize it and make money off it directly.

So, if the written word isn't your thing . . . if conferences, teleseminars or e-courses don't excite you . . . if you are more of an audio or video person – the internet has opened up the entire world to you. Now it's up to you to just open and walk through that door to begin reaping the rewards and making money.

AFTERWORD

So . . . obviously there is a lot of crossover between these last six secrets, but there doesn't have to be. You can choose to implement only one of these secrets, you can choose to keep things as simple as you want, or you can expand them to cover all the suggestions and possible permutations I have suggested.

The point of this whole book is to show you that you *can* do it! It's *easier* than you think! You *can* create a viable internet business quickly with no special technical skills, often without any unique product or service of your own that you have created or offer; without having to carry, deliver, distribute or manage any inventory . . . and without even having to do any bookkeeping. And all this can be done inexpensively – and often, even for free!

So there is no up-front layout of any, or much money for you to get started. All your excuses for not starting . . . for not being able to begin or to do it . . . are eliminated. So – what are you waiting for? Begin! Begin now . . . it's very empowering . . . and could be very lucrative!

EnjOy!

Madeleine

ABOUT THE AUTHOR

Madeleine Kay is the Best Selling Author of *Serendipitously Rich* and *Living Serendipitously.* Adventurist, unconventional success and motivation coach . . . and maverick entrepreneur, she has been featured in *Who's Who of American Women* and *Who's Who in the World.*

Former President and Creative Director of her own advertising and marketing agency, she combines a practical real-life knowledge of business marketing with a hard-earned, nose-to-the-grindstone knowledge of internet marketing . . . to simplify, clarify, consolidate and explain some of the many current simple business opportunities online.

Considered America's leading expert on *serendipity*, she brings the wisdom, passion and playfulness of serendipity sprinkled with her own unique brand of practical, down-to-earth common sense to the world of business to help people get, claim and enjoy the riches they desire.

. . . .

To learn about upcoming events; coaching, consulting
and mentoring assistance; online courses;
and upcoming books, e-books and other "fun stuff"
. . . go to www.madeleinekay.com

OTHER BOOKS BY MADELEINE KAY

Serendipitously Rich . . .
How to Get Delightfully, Delectably, Deliciously Rich
(or anything else you want)
in 7 <u>Ridiculously</u> Easy Steps

Changing *if* I am rich to *when* I am rich has never been simpler . . . or more fun. Refreshingly original and excitingly new, *Serendipitously Rich* shows you how to stop struggling and how to start getting rich (and everything else you want) . . . with effortless ease and unmitigated joy.

Living Serendipitously . . . keeping the wonder alive

A lively and joyful read, *Living Serendipitously* gets you to be an *active dreamer*, who is living your dreams, not just thinking about them. It captures the joyful essence of "the art of living" and shows you how to feel deliciously *alive,* vibrant and happy every day of your life . . . no matter what your circumstances. Einstein said, "There are only two ways to live your life – as though nothing is a miracle or as though everything is a miracle." *Living Serendipitously* aligns us with the *everything.*

Living with Outrageous Joy

Joy is contagious . . . joy is revitalizing . . . joy is what every one of us wants to feel more of in our lives every single day. This charming little gift book will re-ignite that feeling of joy in your life and your passion for living. Playfully inspiring and motivating, *Living with Outrageous Joy* will delight and revitalize you. It will open you up to the joy and adventure of living your life to the fullest every single day . . . unleashing in you that feeling of *aliveness* that so many of us are longing to feel.

The 7 Secrets to Living with Joy and Riches

Joy and riches – we all want lots of both! This delightfully inspiring gift book, with its insightful and pithy sayings, will help you discover how to *savor* your life, not just work at it. *The 7 Secrets to Living with Joy and Riches* will reunite the longings of your soul with the desires of your flesh . . . so you get, claim and enjoy all the joy and riches you desire.

The 12 Myths About Money

Money! We all need it . . . Everyone wants it . . . Nobody wants to admit they care about it . . . And we all wish we had more – Lots more! So why isn't everyone rich? *The 12 Myths About Money* reveals your hidden core beliefs that may be keeping you from becoming rich, and shows you how to instantly replace them with new beliefs that will empower you to think and act like "The Rich" do. The simple *action plan* helps you begin making these new beliefs work for you – now . . . so you can get, claim and enjoy all the riches you desire. (Currently available as e-book at www.madeleinekay.com)

The UMM Factor
(what you need in order to succeed)

Madeleine Kay's groundbreaking book about passion, purpose and prosperity reveals the three things every-one must have in order to succeed. Without all three, it is possible to succeed, but not likely. With them – your success is guaranteed. What are these three magical things? She calls them *The UMM Factor*.

LINKS AND RESOURCES

AWeber – www.aweber.com
Tel. 877-293-2371
(8am – 8pm, EST, M-F & 9am – 5pm, EST, Sat.)
E-mail Marketing Programs

Blogspot (also called Blogger) – www.blogpot.com and www.blogger.com
Online support
Very simple, user-friendly free site for creating blogs

Café Press – www.cafepress.com
Tel. 877-809-1659 (9am – 9pm EST, M-Sat)
Production and Fullfillment Company for Digital-Images on Products

ClickBank – www.clickbank.com
Tel. 208-345-4245 (7am – 6pm MST, M-F)
Affiliate Products and Services (Digital and Download-able)

Commission Junction – www.cj.com
Tel. 800-761-1072 (6am – 5pm PST, M-F)

Affiliate Products and Services (Physical and Digital)

CreateSpace – www.createspace.com
Contact us form at site (8am – 9pm, M-Sat, EST)
Print-on-Demand Division of Amazon for authors, musicians, filmmakers.
Once you open an account with them, you can live chat or phone them or have them phone you, literally instantly. The live support is fabulous!)

Etsy – www.etsy.com – support@etsy.com
Online Buying and Selling Community for Handmade Items

Free Conference Calling – www.freeconferencecalling. com – online support
Hosting, recording and managing free conference calls

Go Daddy – www.godaddy.com
Tel. 480-505-8820 (Live person 24/7)
Websites, Hosting, Domain Names, The Domain Name After Market (TDNAM)

Infinity Publishing – www.infinitypublishing.com
Tel. 877-BUY-BOOK (9am – 5pm, EST. M-F)
Complete Publishing Services for Books, E-books, and Audio Books

Intuit – www.intuit.com
Tel. 877-683-3280 (6am – 5pm PST, M-F)
 Websites, Hosting, QuickBooks, Payment Soluions

Lightning Source – www.lightningsource.com
Tel. 615-213-5815 (9am-5pm, EST)
Print-on-Demand Division of Ingram Distributors

PayDotCom – www.paydotcom.com
Tel. 888-368-0266 (10am – 6pm, EST)
Affiliate Products and Services (Physical and Digital)

PayPal – www.paypal.com
Tel. 888-847-2747
Payment Service

Oversee – www.oversee.net
Tel. 213-408-0080 (Corporate office in Los Angeles),
954-861-3500 (Florida office of Moniker, division of
Oversee that organized The DomainFest live auction)
www.snapnames.com
Tel. 503-219-9990 (Oregon office of Snap Names
Division). Domain Management and Sale Company

Sedo – www.sedo.com
Tel. 617-499-7200 (9am – 6pm EST)
Domain Names for Sale Internationally

Word Press – www.wordpress.com – 24/7 forum support
Hosted free blogging site

FYI – Just as CreateSpace offers live support once you've
signed up and opened an account with them, it is possible
that some of the sites listed above may also provide live

support once you've signed up with them. If live support is important to you, this is something you may want to check out prior to signing up.

. . . .

Madeleine Kay is the Founder of the Serendipity Day
Holiday, celebrated August 18th . You can learn about this
exciting new event and how to live serendipitously all year
long at . . . www.serendipitydayholiday.com

Browse serendipity wearables, carryables,
and other "fun stuff" at The Serendipity Shoppe at . . .
www.cafepress.com/serendip_shoppe

Receive a FREE copy of The Serendipity Handbook at . . .
www.facebook.com/serendipityday.

Also receive a FREE 7 Myths about money E-course and
E-book at . . . www.madeleinekay.com

. . . .

. . . .

Follow Madeleine's blog online at
www.madeleinekaylive.com

For personal one-on-one coaching or consulting,
contact Madeleine at . . . www.madeleinekay.com

. . . .

Notes

Notes

Notes

Notes

Notes

www.ingramcontent.com/pod-product-compliance
Lightning Source LLC
Chambersburg PA
CBHW051256050326
40689CB00007B/1222